NECESSARY FIRE

NECESSARY

FIRE

BLACK LAWRENCE PRESS

KMA SULLIVAN

POEMS

WWW.BLACKLAWRENCE.COM

Executive Editor: Diane Goettel
Book and Cover Design: Alban Fischer
Cover artwork: © Christina McPhee, Inversion 14, *chromogenic print, 2012*
Interior artwork: ©Christina McPhee Inversion 17, *digital photograph, 2012.*
Both images from the photographic series "Inversions"
are used with the permission of the artist.

Copyright © 2015 KMA Sullivan
ISBN: 978-1-62557-932-4

Black Lawrence Press
326 Bigham Street
Pittsburgh, PA 15211

Published 2015 by Black Lawrence Press
Printed in the United States

FOR DANIEL

CONTENTS

THRASHING

I'll start with the way my youngest rubs the center of my forehead
with his thumb when I need to calm down or he's about to ask for an
advance on his allowance so he can buy weed or a permanent marker
for Emily who will cover his forearms in viney tattoos and has invited
him to work the river with her this summer so he can earn money by
renting inner tubes to country boys who earn county medals wrestling
other boys in leotards on mats but would break and bloody my son for
rocking rayon genie pants and hemp bracelets and loving another boy
on the mouth the way we were meant to soft and hard and aiming for
each other's center so we might for a moment pretend we aren't alone
as we thrash and thrash and thrash in this world of lips and blood
and rivers.

FEAR COMES

when you kneel bedside, head resting against
your mother who is unconscious but still in pain,
you realize what you dread and hope are the same—

the son you loved past addiction—past counties full
of lies—offers his hand through bulletproof glass
but you're not sure you know his fingers anymore

while your father, who hunted wild mushrooms
and taught you how to find Cassiopeia in November sky,
no longer understands the cable bill.

When fear comes it creeps around cedar siding,
peers in windows, lips to sill, eyes
so sad and wild even priests leave town.

WAITING FOR PANGAEA

2.5 centimeters per year is the average rate human fingernails grow. Earth's continents move with similar breathlessness. Floating on molten rock that churns, plates slam into and separate from one another with a force that pushes the Himalayas toward ever-thinning air and, one day, will break California into shallows. Even galaxies stray from their centers. I wonder if the Milky Way occasionally longs for days before the singular blast that made family reunions more difficult to plan. Scientists don't seem worried. They say dark matter is the glue that binds the cosmos to itself. It will hold. I wonder if that's just an idea out of the academy to explain what we don't understand? Like why there were no photographs of my adopted children on the walls of the foster home where they'd lived for three years. Like why one of my sons hid canned peaches behind toilet paper in the bathroom closet before he was arrested for forgery and shoplifting. Like why my daughter didn't touch my hair with her hands until I'd been her mother for two years and why her earlier mothers never allowed her to run.

GROWN TANGLED

Do the scales on a pangolin ever let go, walk off
by themselves and look for daffodils? They might
find a new home in a wild clutch of bulbs, decide to protect
fluted petals from the rain or stay a little while

then move on in search of tiger lilies and trumpet vines
grown tangled in Eastern Hemlock. Married at 22,
I missed loneliness and traveled straight to footed pajamas,
cello recitals, and 3D models of Jamestown.

Christmas stockings are cross stitched with colored silk,
photo albums are decorated with landscape die cuts and balloon
stickers. I bake carrot cake and chocolate cake and strawberry-iced
vanilla cake for birthday dinners. My youngest chooses

blueberry cobbler for his candles. Lop-eared rabbits,
black bear hamsters, and chinchillas in specialty colors fill empty spaces.
These days I wonder about emptiness. What happens
in a place so quiet not even a popped cello string can ring out?

NO MORE

When was the last time
I rocked you to sleep
in a warm dark room,
your milky breath on my face?

What day, what hour, what minute
marked the end?

Did I kiss your palm, stroke
your toenail with my thumb,
watch your eyelashes sink and float
and finally come to rest on the pink
of your cheek?

Or, anxious to wipe linoleum counters,
start the evening soup, sit
at my writing table,
was I waiting to let you go?

For the sweetness that filled me,
that will never come again,
I hope I lingered.

DOES ANYONE NEED SAVING?

Wonder Woman, red cape trailing, orders an iced mocha
at the coffee shop counter. She sips from the side
of the plastic cup. *Straws cause creases,* she says, touching
her upper lip and looking at a middle-aged
woman who stops drinking her ice water.

But hey, I'm here to save the day.
        Does anyone need saving?

A customer asks Wonder Woman
if she can convince the shop owner to talk
more softly so she can eat her banana nut muffin
and have a quiet minute. *Sorry,*
that's above my pay grade, she says.

A man whose wife died a year ago, stands
in the pastry line. He asks her if she can find a new mother
for his boys—one who knows how to make potato salad
with mustard. *No,* says Wonder Woman, *but I can show you*
how my Lasso of Truth attaches to my gold belt.

The little girl who's been pulling on a corner
of the superhero's polyester cape lets go.

Wonder Woman takes another sip of her mocha,
pushes the screen door open and strides into the afternoon,
her red shin guards skim the top of her Air Jordans.

WONDERING ABOUT THE CANCELLATION PENALTY ON MY CELL PHONE CONTRACT

You call again because the beer didn't work and the pills didn't work and neither did the water syringe. You call because you have a twelve-year-old girl who is 4'10" and 75 pounds and can't speak. I sit in my chair, the one with the high back and the hunter green upholstery and I think about 5-bean soup. It's warm and thick and salty. You call because the child who can't speak can bite and punch and does bite and punch until both of you are purple and yellow and wet. I think about reheating my soup but if I put it in a saucepan it will bubble at the edges and burn at the bottom because sometimes when you call I forget about soup. You call again because the child's father is cleaning another pool and having his skin checked at the dermatologist and talking to his son's probation officer because his son, who is nineteen, also bites and punches. I remember when that boy used to sing but that was before the bleeding cross tattoo and the restraining order and the line of safety pins piercing his left cheek, before he was returned to his mother, the heroin addict, who isn't you. And I take your call because I remember you holding that boy and reading *Are You My Mother?* It's OK if my soup burns. You call again because the silent child, your daughter, is shitting herself in school and she won't sit still long enough for the ambulatory EEG to be attached to her scalp and the neurologist says he's done with your case. I wonder how he can do that, just let you go. But then you tell me about how you found his car in the "Doctor's Only" section of the parking lot and smashed the headlights of his *Infiniti* with your tire iron.

TUESDAY MORNING AT THE POST OFFICE

I make sense of things—
an empty condom box on the curb
tells of hope for a boy in his backseat trying,
a whistling man seeks warmth in the mailbox lobby,
a woman who danced for Balanchine walks
with two canes as she sends brightly colored packages to friends,
pointed breasts emerge from the postal clerk,
her diamond earlobes, wispy bangs, and balding forehead
compete with broken pink fingernails.

ADOPTED LATE

Two years you've been my daughter
and today you decide it's okay to touch
my hair with the brush, with your hands.
It took my return from a four-day absence
for you to finally stake your claim.

Your younger brothers, who emerged
from my body, huge and gasping,
have always known that they can kiss
my chin, stroke the hair on my arm,
rest their heads in my lap, make demands.

You've been watching from a distance.

So small, cocooned in your Winnie-the-Pooh
blanket; I've been looking for you and I'll keep looking
even when you try to disappear.
I want to hear you talk about pink striped skies
and cockatiels with speckled tails
and all the people you remember.

NIGHT MEDICINE

capillaries expand
on surface skin
stinging fire worries forehead
travels
to chest, arms, thighs
you wet washcloths
place them with care
after 27 years
I still look for you
to cool me
when I wake from dreams
burning

FAMILY REUNION

I.   Front teeth gone along with your ability to choose a brand
      of shampoo. A woman, a friend, has taken you in. Her ten-
      year-old makes sure you have bologna sandwiches so that low
      blood sugar and an insulin overdose don't land you in the
      ICU again.

II.   Five different kinds of meatballs and a karaoke d.j. who
      didn't play too long were the highlights of the day you
      married your third wife who came with two fat children and
      a mother who looked like a man. Not even text messages can
      get out of West Virginia.

III. With only a crucifix over the bed to protect her, your
      mother's love, like her babies, came quickly and almost
      spent. In a world of Irish whiskey, without hope or ice, where
      lessons learned are few and buried, no wonder they thought
      you were a mistake.

IV.   Not everyone wants to keel on her first sail. Boat tipped,
      sail might catch water, suck you under. You've already been
      burned by jib sheets, your mother's broken rudder, and a
      grandfather who drinks wine out of a 7-Eleven Big Gulp.

V.   The fireplace licks and burns with colored flames from birthday wrapping paper and scissor-curled ribbon. Like a bead of grease on a hot iron skillet, you spit and dance and wait for milky batter to cover you.

VI.   You sit in the red vinyl restaurant booth the way a trout lies in the sink: a few shudders belying readiness to lose head and tail, waiting to be boned. You and the trout share a glassy unfocused eye.

VII.   You are the buzz of cicadas in the dark, the eyelash never beyond my peripheral vision, the clicking of the heater when it decides to turn on. You, the child who isn't here, never bigger than a cashew. A girl, I insist. With five babies grown, why does the wish of you linger?

VIII. Dust blinks and rises off pine boards. Feet touch wood grain to feel warmth through calluses, through doubt. Ankles ache, knees quiver, neck bends. You call. You call. And you don't. At the end of the day even light moves backward.

HAVE I BEEN SAVED?

I've been wondering because the snow
                              is pink today   and

        living in southwest Virginia makes me think about slathering
mustard on my pretzel.
                        The heart of things
            is that I can never find socks that match
and
                              people who drive into snow drifts
            have instructions I don't understand   and

sometimes the dog shitting in the living room is an understatement.

            But you like the way my hips glow in the blue pulse
                              of your laptop
and you inside me

        is the only way I want to finish the day.

SMALL, THEY SAID

The white on the film
a golf ball, a walnut, a mass
that pulled memory from love,
splitting time into then and now,
cleaving you from yourself.

Was it small like a pencil? A nickel?
The two-word diagnosis in their file:
anaplastic astrocytoma?
Or small like a smile that opens the day,
a pink fist that breaks into air?

No, it was small like a magician's wand—
shutting the mouth, holding all eyes,
sinking before a quiet gasp—
you the Vanishing Lady,
us left holding the box.

NIGHT AIR

If I breathe deep I can make it through this dark.
Drop my arms from my chest, suck
air until my stomach fills, I can make it through
this hollow. The children are in bed.
The night valley begins to shudder. The rhythm
of tree frogs presses at my back. Before they burrow,
cicadas drown out whippoorwills' call. Maybe tonight,
the coyotes will rest on the hills without howling.

SONG FOR
MY MOTHER

I will play for you
until we walk out of the woods
and Mandelbrot's edges seep into day.

I will play for you
until the surgeon offers hope
and tomorrow is diminished
and piano keys are stripped to the glue.

I will play for you
until fingernails are clean
and visiting hours are over
and our clothes are all that hold us together.

I will play for you
until words are gone
and your tongue searches for bread
and oxygen tubes tangle on the sheet.

And I will keep playing
when yellow fills your eye
and nightgowns must be slit.

I will play for you
until the pastor comes
and cherry blossoms burst
and Chopin is no longer about the rain.

And I won't stop playing
when bruised skin is washed
and the healer sings farewell
and even the mail is more that I can carry.

I will play for you
until the wooden box is ash
and the photos are the story
and your love lies over the hole he has dug for you both.

I will play for you
until salt breezes stir
and aspen leaves tremble
and my heart considers the buoyant fractal of starlings.

CONSIDERING ANTIQUES AND CURIOSITIES

In the back room of Foster's Miscellany,
cardboard Glinda asks *Are you a good
witch or a bad witch?* as she rests
between a framed flying lizard and whorehouse
coins. *Good for one screw, one stogie, one whiskey*
announces the Gold Rush remnant. It turns out
the coins are replicas, not good for anything
but flexing the imagination
of a middle-aged woman. The lizard,
glued to board and under glass, reveals sails
of pleated skin, a long graceful tail,
and a desiccated body that used to glide
through the heated air of Papua New Guinea.

YOU WONDER

You wonder why you're the only survivor of your original home, why, unlike your brother, you don't stare at restaurant menus, trying to remember the location of the nearest methadone clinic.

You, eight years old, sat in the corner of the living room reading a volume of *The Golden Home and High School Encyclopedia* your aunt, the nun, brought the previous Easter, while your brother knocked up his girlfriend on the couch in the garage.

Why, unlike your sister, you don't wait until you're drunk to make family phone calls on Thanksgiving, and why you don't visit your father's grave each month to kiss the cemetery stone.

You, at eleven, sat with your mother in the dark-paneled waiting room as doctors tried to prevent your father's 48-year-old liver from failing. You remember walking back from the snack area to find your father had died while you were getting a Three Musketeers Bar.

You wonder how you can be a father, having seen so little of the job, other than how your own father had balanced on a bar stool at Collin's Tavern until you got tired of waiting in the car with your plastic army men and went inside for a glass of ginger ale.

You, the only person I know who knows by the muscles in his back that cabbage is the heaviest vegetable by the bushel and that banding radishes takes twice as long in the rain.

And you wonder how you can be a husband and be loved for just the brown of your eyes and the freckles on your arms, which is sometimes all you believe you bring to our family table.

You, who threw the *West Springfield Daily Record* as you walked local streets before school and later cleared banquet tables at The Coliseum with those freckled arms and large-knuckled hands so you could buy the family's first car and drive your mother to the Shop & Save, so she could bring home orange juice and American cheese and Wonder Bread.

JUNE SERVICE

my sister doesn't show

transistors in her teeth

whisper of tainted reception sandwiches

my brother arrives late   his son needs a new tie

my mother's thin gold band on the altar

in a pottery urn with ashes and bone

delphinium will break your heart

says the clerk at Bayberry Gardens

my father digs the hole   in the family plot

under an ancient tree

red clay rings chinos

dyes tennis shoes

a friend looks on and measures depth

a kind of showing up

it starts to rain through rough limbs and pointed needles

but not before my uncle   dulled by wine in a travel coffee mug

sprays mosquito repellant

past children's necks into eyes

even the pitch pine weeps

WHY MY SOCKS DON'T MATCH

Dishes sit in the sink; the morning's oatmeal mingles
with last night's rice pot. I will let them enjoy one another
while I read a poem by the young writer
who seems to know what I think about
when I wash my hair and let the water
flow across my eyes and chin. Three baskets of laundry
sit at the foot of my bed, a stack of papers that needs
grading balances on my desk, but the cockatiel is singing,
playing for himself the songs of all the birds he can hear.

I want to wonder about wonder:
how many fireflies I saw last night
and did some of the suspended lovers
find each other; how the cicada corpse hangs
upside down in the doorway, ready to protect us from intruders;
why the blue tasseled hat that warms my youngest
announces the ebullience of his spirit and why
the word ebullience makes me think of driftwood
and diving horsehead seals and dune grass purpled
with beach pea flowers.

So I might take a look at the mail, call the math teacher
who doesn't explain quadratic equations very well,

match a sock or two. More likely
I'll rub the feet of my youngest son
as we watch a video on Indian balloon frogs
or the history of Islamic diving bells
while I breathe in this moment
and the next.

THIS LIFE

On my own a bottle of wine lasts a week, a box of chocolate cookies three days. On Irving Street, on the way to coffee and a cranberry scone, I pass a man on his way to work. He is earnest, small. I tower over him. Think relativity, proportion, a rush toward illusion. His iPod does not make him taller. These boots don't make me thinner. I wonder how many times Anna will razor her thighs, cut internal places before reassurance covers her, how many times Gary will text *it's not my fault* before he sees that it is, how many times I will say *No baby, adopting stray kittens is not the same as taking your bipolar meds.* Sometimes the rain is inside. It waters my ribs, spleen, the arteries that are hardening. Showers drip from the clouds in my throat, no biplanes needed to seed this mist. Even the cat, shaved because of matting, has lost herself. This life, so much thrashing. These hands have held worlds, only you can hold me, make me small.

I DON'T VISIT GRAVESTONES

I don't want to trace the J of my mother's
name in carved granite, fingering the curve
just so, or see how my father's companion

stone sits ready for the final date.
I'm not going to feel the ivy that's begun to crawl
around beveled corners, pulling her marker

further into the ground, mixing her leftovers
with other graves, other absences.
I don't need to see how the pitch pine hangs

over the family plot or smell the lilies of the valley
that still bloom in May, planted
by my grandmother for her parents.

And I won't touch the wooden cross
that stands in the middle of this granite garden.
In Virginia, clinic workers are required to count

body parts of fetuses that have been aborted.
I wonder about cataloging severed bits no longer
connected to fear or expectation.

Once the body's in pieces, I say:
cross yourself and move on.

NOTE TO A
YOUNG FRIEND

I won't say I love you.
You write these words to me
on notes you pass in class.
Love is still a county fair for you,
apple pie for breakfast, all-night
pizza delivery, a candy cane tree.

There's a young woman who'll show
you soon that those words
come with oceans to swim
and spiders that can't be sprayed.

I've already crossed too many oceans.
I need to keep my feet on shore
for a while. But stand with me
at the edge of the low-tide lagoon.

We can squish sand through our toes,
call out to the horsehead seal
when she surfaces, dig
for phosphorous at water's edge.

That is more than enough,
and more than either of us expected.

MOIST

It's strange this unzipping
spilling intestines and longing
onto the card table
hoping someone might care
might get it
who we are
under the subcutaneous fat
so puzzling and obvious
just touching really
that's what we want
that and a cranberry scone
and maybe a clean towel
one that doesn't smell from August
because after the shower
we leave bits of ourselves
that grow and stink in the heat
as the cotton loops hang on the hook
we've done what we can
to get clean
to rid ourselves of desire
for new lovers
who would press their lips
into our eyes

and find a freshness
that would leave
the August towels alone
but there is no new day
no immaculate extension
the decay is upon us
and has been since day two
so we sit at the table
put our guts back in the bag
zip up our bellies
and listen to the towels
spin in the dryer

THE HORSE HAS GOTTEN OUT AGAIN

having pushed through the wood
that pretends to hold him
he chews the chickweed
outside my window

his head fills the glass
he is content
to drag his hoof across roots
when he carries me
under the lowest limb
so I have to choose between ducking
and a smack in the face

I learned early to sleep in the cold
pine burns hot and fast in the stove
but can't bend around corners
no warmth found where I slept

many mornings found me
staring out the window
watching my father's tail light recede
long before thrush called in the day

just before I would turn away
to stoke the nearly dead ash

these days I burn from the inside
and find myself
both horse and jockey
pulling at the leather

at once soft mouth and hard hand
I notice other riders
see their skillful methods
admire their colored silk
there seem to be rules to follow
paths cut by previous boldness
a wildness let loose
that had seen earlier bottling

so many observers with large hats
sit in the stands
their hopes and expectations shout down
on the elliptical dirt

I take it in but don't understand
the myriad voices
I am trying to win
to be worthy of all this color
but mostly
I just want to run

WHEN MY
FATHER FALLS

like an old tree
cut at the stump
he will grow taller
on the way down
no longer bowed at the knee
by childhood rickets
and a mother meant
for other than baking
even bones can straighten
with memory
that master of revision
and why not?
can't we choose what to remember?
tapping swamp maples
with dowel and pail
the way he rode the waves
all the way to the stones
the way he loved as an old man
gentle
the way he loved as a husband
cutting sod to plant a weeping cherry
like the one in full bloom
when his wife passed

and he knelt by the bed
and read a poem
about the just passing
without a sound

FIRST-PERSON SHOOTER

I was there not like they were there the eagle scout who stopped the door with a table and his femoral artery the student who lay quiet under the wounds of another the teacher who still can't read stories by sad students who write of extension cords and tall trees but I was there playing tennis as other people's children were dying I remember a truck with a megaphone a cell phone finally answered at court change it was over by then no one knew even the shooter was dead I remember running my husband locked in his office one building away from the early kills that turned out to be a warm up act three of our children locked in their schools our oldest safe in another town but my eleven-year-old was sick at home while other children were shot for showing up to class so I ran with the campus minister both of us grabbing tennis bags, racquets, and shoes he to his students the teachers the university that needed I didn't give a fuck about any of them I drove past fields and fences cows and sharpshooters waiting sirens and lights in my rearview one child that's all one child the world when I got home that child on the couch with a blanket the dog curled beside a glass of orange juice confused by a mother's kiss my rough hold interrupting his video game

CIRCADIAN RHYTHM

Forty-nine years of paying
attention, I've learned
a few things.

But I still don't know
why, when you sleep,
the morning glories
close their petals as if
they are no longer needed.

A MOTHER'S CRIME

I wasn't fragile until I saw
your smile, felt your hands grasp
my hair, neck, breast.

But your toes that once curled
at our hello, the voice that sought
me in the house, the park, the night,
has turned into eyes that roll
at the sound of my breathing.

How did I become too rank
to touch, embarrassing merely
by the way I eat crackers
or laugh on the phone?

Birthday cupcakes for class
are no longer required
and neither is my mouth or face.
Now, when you raise your chin
it is not to ask for a kiss.

But the boy is still there
behind lashes and lids.

You might yet nod or smile
my way or even rest your head
in my lap

I lurk in doorways, waiting
for one more moment with you
before you break into the man
you have almost become.

CAREFUL

I stand at the sink
snapping the tail
off a lobster
a strange satisfaction
as I crack the shell
clean the thread of waste
a friend
I'm getting to know again
stands at the cutting board
addressing the mushrooms
in thin slices
talks of his quiet days
when he walks his dog
where he puts his shoes
his addiction
to internet porn
chat rooms
where men vie for attention
from Romanian women
while his careful wife
steps in and out of the kitchen

wondering if she can help
we look up
and nod

PLAYING TENNIS WITH OLD MEN

Contemplating corners our opponent serves deep just outside the line. He throws up another. With so much riding on the serve it's only fair he should have a second chance. Like when he married a woman of generous spirit after his first wife borrowed their daughter's underwire and hung herself in the afternoon. I still remember how he played *Abiyoyo* on the Baldwin upright and how his first wife sang, her green eyes alive and darting. Server's partner crouches a racquet length from the net. He appraises service box, trying to predict the return. Knee brace steadies bowed legs just as his gentle wife with the off-center eye has steadied him all these years. He's hoping for a short overhead or weak passing shot so he can slam it back and later bring his wife some of the fire that has burned through 53 years of sharing cotton covered pillows. My partner, my father, calls the second serve: *Good*. With legs as thin as a yard flamingo's, his balance unsteady, he returns it down the line. Not even tai chi in a church basement can return his wife from the ground. But he's back on the court as he is back at his writing desk, fielding editors' rejections with reflexes enough to save today's rally from a bad bounce off soft clay.

I BELIEVE IN SANDWICHES

chicken and onion
lettuce and cheese
anything that fits
between two pieces of toast
and might give
my mouth something to do
my mind something to think
how about pickles
how they are made
but that leads me to brine
which is what is leaking
out in the blinking
and an unconscious waving
of my left hand
stop I gesture
but to whom
to the memory of what I've already done?
too late says the chicken
I'm already laid out in mayonnaise
and you are about to bite me
again

THESE DAYS ARE LONG WITHOUT YOU

The top of the locust tree bickers
with itself. That fills a minute.
Morning fog refuses to burn off
so wren and chickadee doze
in bush, on branch, as young oaks gossip.
Ancient pitch pine unmoved,
needles hang in the air.
The hammock, made for two,
twists on itself. Steel ring holds,
one frayed cord no longer carries its load.
I untangle the hammock, swing for a while,
wait for quail to rustle in the undergrowth,
my whole body counting the seconds.

SEARCHING FOR ANSWERS IN THE FEMININE HYGIENE AISLE

When I get to the grocery store, I stand
under the vapor spray in the vegetable case.

The recording of a distant storm plays
as water drizzles down variegated skins.

I push my cart to the feminine hygiene
aisle where I finger my bottle of Nexxus Humectress.

O! *Magazine* assures me that women over 40
can wear long hair if it's properly conditioned.

My eyes try to focus on pink and white packaged
panty liners and pads. When does coverage

for mid-cycle spotting turn into a daily
necessity because the plumbing is giving

out altogether? I want to get back
to the vegetables and rest with the eggplant.

YOU ARE MY
FAVORITE ERECTION

I'm tired of waiting for goodnight kisses that don't come. Can't you hear my waist, the dip behind my ear wondering where you are? Can't you feel me beneath your ribs, in the tendons, in your gums? But taxes need to be figured. Another article needs writing. The dog has to go to the vet. Our oldest is trying to hold down a job, hold back his pit bull from mauling his girlfriend, who is in her 34th week. Another son, at art school for a while, finally moved out of the bedroom upstairs, but grocery money seems hard to hold onto between poker games. The 4th child, the one who reads Kafka for fun, can't manage to graduate with his high school class. But what we have built with Legos and Scrabble, our hopes, our teeth, is enough to end each day thanking the sheets for each other. So forget the mail, the mower, the children. Test this pillow with me. We have some building to do.

ANT LOVE

is tiny love
shorter than grass
on the way to a picnic
hoping for a watermelon rind
it can carry

SATURDAY

In the morning you move your tongue over me
       like I'm a linen canvas
              and you work in oils.
     Cadmium red and cerulean blue take days to dry.

My body is a county fair.
         You're a regular at all the two and four ticket booths.
     (shoot the duck, spin the tea cup,
                kiss the middle-aged wife)
        Pink cotton candy melts in your mouth. I appreciate
        the tractor pull.

You are a zombie and I'm the last fresh ankle.

We watch *Wolverine* on DVD.
        You tell me I could pretend to make love to him.
    I say, *Baby, if I had sex with Hugh Jackman*
        I'd have to imagine your fingers,
             your mouth, your eyes to come.

You discover new ways to help me
              wash my hair, take a nap,
      brush my teeth at the bathroom sink.

I wonder out loud if we've mapped all our caves,
      discovered all the radiant creatures that dwell in the dark.

There's only one way to find out, you say.

You strap on your headlamp,
        pack chicken salad sandwiches,
    and go spelunking the rest of the day.

FLOATING

my youngest knew
how to swish sequined tail
splash bathwater
over tile let it flow
down sheetrock
yards of fuchsia fabric
as good as scales
and skin

inches below surface
he still holds his breath
watches bubbles
move toward open air
where his fluid worlds
might open
and combine with
the oxygen of others

like Ariel he collects trinkets
Japanese fans, Hindu gods,
a young Buddha
rest on his dresser
beside homemade incense

as a good luck dragon
carved into blue quartz
glows through photos

of a boy who jumped
into the Hudson River
when his lovemaking
was turned into entertainment,
and a fifteen-year-old
on life support after hanging himself,
two other boys beaten and raped
until they confessed

for my boy I want an ocean
so free he can ride underwater
rivers without fear of riptide
float on the current of himself
where the sound of rushing
water means mermaids
are about to sing

FOR HIM I WOULD PAWN MY METAL

Ruby-eyed snake pin with diamonds at the head passed down through granddaughters. A ring of tanzanite and white gold that marked nine months spent soothing my mother. I'd sell these and my gold bangle, the one with Ceylon sapphires clear blue like the sky, for one more day of contentment, an iced coffee, his favorite burrito. But he has days when he sleeps through the sun, when dishes in the sink weigh more than the stove, when every bar of soap calls his name until his wrists shine red. And money won't change that. Neither will love. He is not the one I rest on at night, not the one who kisses my hips as if they were ripe plums. But he has a place in me still, hidden from the cares of the day, the children's report cards, the smell of the dog who still shits on the floor. He brings life to a corner of me that's been choked with laundered rags and brings music I'd forgotten how to sway to. He's not the one I'll grow old with, not the one in whose eyes I will always be young, but I hope tomorrow and tomorrow we'll still be walking together and talking about nothing and everything and nothing.

HOLE

cereal bars, a stand in for affection
me, a placeholder for something better.
that I tether myself to someone so careless
with the hearts of others when mine dissolves
in milk, renders me unrecognizable
to friends, my rearview mirror

a wallowing no one has been able to sound
you are fascinated by the way hair grows
on the knuckle of your big toe
if I threw a pebble, a piano, myself
into your watery mouth would offerings
ever sink far enough to gather?

like the karst under Mountain Lake,
your holes are hidden and shifting
people cast mattresses, trash, bags of cement
into the lake to block the drain of summer
but only movement of the earth itself
can stop this emptying

SPRING TIDE

You have broken the back of me.
My ballast is gone. It's on the ocean floor
with the tubeworms and giant clams.

The keel that has steadied me in so many gales,
cannot extend. I take on water.
Now just a raft of wooden doors and sandwiches and twine,
I reach into the cold and pull up the survivors
who still need to rest on what is left.

What you've forgotten, or don't even care to know:
I come from the sea.

As a girl, I looked for the surf in my face,
the chance to push into the airless blue
and surge to the surface gasping.

I searched for the biggest swell,
the one with lace at the top
telling me it's about to crash down,
and I'd ride that fucker all the way in.

VIRIDIAN

how the head is held
by the neck
says so much
about our shutters and hinges
what we are willing to see
where the limits are
of our bearing
some old men will look
directly at the cunt
of a bonneted nude
some look down and away
I'm tired of looking
at the center of you
trying to understand what you say
needs to be understood
I long for a patina
a heart
that is another kind of green
I don't ask for fairness
which is different from every view
but I wouldn't mind a release
a cushion of teeth
yours

might provide a resting place
for what is tired in me
it's odd
how each loss feels fresh
when so much is repeated
these copper tiles
offer the same tripping edge
my toe catches every time

REALITY TV

it turns out
unpeeling myself
is easy
I accept
that this was not always the case
there were years
of wax seals
on blueberry jam
and sap
boiled to syrup
40 to 1
but now
governors hold
press conferences
on true love
that lead them
away from sons
and office
in this time
what is hard
about confessing
to love of cock
and swallowing

pills that drain
me of panic
and compassion
when everyone lives
to hear the howling

WITNESS

Bridges should be watched. A slip
of design and steel plates fight themselves.
They ripple in the wind, break into pieces,
drown their bits in Puget Sound
on camera as if on cue.

I see a friend stare at his hands
made pink from scalding. Persistent voices
call for a burning after he has touched
the kitchen trash, a gas nozzle,
yesterday's jeans.

In February my sister moves, throws
her daughter and a few bags in the car,
leaves the rest. She travels to Seattle, Asheville,
Boulder, New South Wales so that her mind
might begin again.

My oldest son glistens on football field and wrestling mat,
his focus aligned and humming. But his thoughts, trained
by early abandonment, twist and pull. His breaking
will come from the inside and, like the camera man
on the far side of the bridge, all I can do is watch.

I MET JESUS TODAY

He didn't have shoelaces
dental floss
a cell phone charger
a woman with a plastic fork
follows him
later her wrists
strapped down
for what she wants
to do with her fork
on other people's skin

I'm in a room
with no door
no off switch
for the overhead light
shadows under my skin
at the back of my eye
might be quiet
in some permanent dark

I met Jesus today

in morning group
I told plastic chairs
I want to be quartered
left leg goes to Lamu
right arm to Salt Lake City
head and torso to Phoenix
I could be reborn
fly to Africa
pick up my femur
and its knee cap

now I have to stay until Wednesday

take new pills
find chapstick
wear hoodies without strings
figure out
what to say to friends
the ones who show up
the ones who don't
call my mother
listen to her breathe

FIRST BORN

The light of my star
Has been wrung for you.

Shine.

SOME MORNINGS

On mornings when the peony's head droops,
spider webs own doorway corners,
I look at photos where only I am a stranger.
Loose skin wants to be filled with pieces
of me I left on Route 6 between Truro and Provincetown.
Seventeen, top down, singing with Joe Walsh,
too many Long Island iced teas to know I was
driving too fast, living fast enough to turn left
at the green sign onto a road where I am forty-nine
with five children and a grandchild on the way.

THIS IS NEW
THIS ABSENCE

Even the air has changed.
Like a squid caught for bait
gasping for breath on the dock,
I wish I could turn colors in the dying,
become food for some larger fish.
Instead I stare at the solitaire on my phone,
hoping for a six of spades
so the five of diamonds might reveal
something random and good.

LEFT STAGGERING

I knew a mother who went to the store
for orange juice and just kept driving—
past the karate studio, the soccer field,
her husband's understanding.

She left in search of a moment, a closet
without wrapping paper and curling ribbon, a table
not covered in permission slips for the zoo,
a room with a quiet shelf.

Three sons, a daughter lost early, a husband
who liked the way she cooked macaroni, left her wanting
salt breeze on her face. The wind might fill her again
in places gutted by church hospitality committees
and Boy Scout merit badge ceremonies.

A moon or two wandering Pamet River marshland,
listening to watercress push through the spring bed,
smelling layers of leaf and moss and decaying limbs,
watching wild turkey chaperone young ones

who stagger up the hill, left her ready to return
to the touch of a small hand on her arm. But by then
she'd been replaced by a Swedish au pair
who also knew how to cook noodles.

RIVER'S BEND

My abdomen is bloated with blood
maybe for the last time. Should I revel
in the numb ache of this fullness?

So much longing has been carried with the ebb
and flow from this river basin:
our babies conceived who refused to be born,
our babies conceived who came crushing into this world.

What happens when the river ends?
Recently it's been seeping through my pants,
onto the chair, down my leg, onto the floor. I keep trying
to spell the word: *exaguinate, ecsagunate, exsanguinate,*
and have to settle for bloodletting.

My doctor has three words: global endometrial ablation.
Is that like world-wide elation? Whole earth meditation?
Four different pills, an opium suppository, three days in bed,
    and a balloon on fire—
it's hard to tell.

And when only the riverbed remains, what will I be?
The dry part of a woman doesn't seem like woman at all.

IN MONTECAVOLO, ITALY THERE IS A BANK FILLED WITH CHEESE

80 pound wheels of parmesan are collateral for loans
on supplies and equipment and a mistress's lavender soap.
Deposited in cooled chambers until ripe, tapped for proper aging,
discarded if centers are rotten. There is hollowness in that sound.

I'd like to deposit my grief somewhere. Release
the weight of it. My knuckles can't keep a scab. Grief rings
my neck in brass pushing my clavicle down, down. Bones
are shifting and will soon find a permanent setting.

But if I could put some of the things I know
in a vault, let them age on their own,
take a loan for two gingerbread lattes
and a new pink scarf, it would be a win all around.

I choose the evening I saw my oldest son through bulletproof glass.
Orange jumpsuit and shackles, the hard look in his eye, a gauntness
to his cheek. I remember looking at the skin on the back of his hands,
and realizing that my heart, too, had thinned.

OPENING SONG

Two days of sun and the morning explodes
with birdsong. Whippoorwill finishes
as my mind reaches for the early light
that stretches up the Pamet River. No worries,
goldfinch and song sparrow take up the day.
Chickadee and crow fill left over spaces.

Yesterday it was sunny after two weeks of rain.
Why no song until today? Perhaps birds too
are cautious, nervous when emerging from sad days.

Regaining my footing has been slow. A son in jail,
my mother early in the ground, my sister untouched
by reason, reasons to stay in bed have been piling up.
This morning, like so many before, you back into me
so that our bodies form a single curve. You wait
for my arm around your waist. I may yet sing tomorrow.

NECESSARY FIRE

Steam explodes from coals that burn orange-red
just before seawater lays waste to beach fire.
Three boys, ten-years-old, dance in steam and sputter
as they wave metal forks recently warm from marshmallow
torches. I imagine a dance like this to choose
spear throwers for the bison hunt at dawn. Later,
as the meat is roasting in the fire pit, one of the quiet
boys might scratch ochre on stone to tell the story.

You used to be one of those wild boys: climbing electric
towers, holding lit fireworks by the tips of your fingers,
shooting tennis balls from a bazooka made of duct tape, lighter
fluid and Schlitz beer cans. On warm evenings in June
you wove your bike back and forth through DDT clouds
spewing from the back of the mosquito truck.

Our own boys, not allowed to hold explosive devices, or climb
electrified fences, or fly through poisonous gas, have found
other ways to taste the inside of their mouths. A ring of flame
out of Antonio Banderas cologne has burned evidence
into our back porch. You have explained to me that sometimes
passing cars beg to be hit by water balloons. Two of our sons

coated each other's hands with bug spray, put a match to the shine,
and waited to see which one would let his own palm burn.

I remember you swinging on the porch in the dark
with our three-year-old. The night crackled with heat lightning
as it shot across Ellett Valley. He, our own summer storm,
was as transfixed then as when you cupped your hand
and showed him the lightning bug inside. I see now,
you were getting him ready. Ready to hold lightning, ignite
perfume, and dance on the coals of a dying beach fire.

STAND HERE IF
YOU LIKE

listen to my story if you like
but you won't understand
the canned peaches
hidden behind toilet paper
or the child who keeps tags
on her clothes to show others
she is loved
you won't feel the snot
that runs down her lip and chin
because her face doesn't feel anything anymore
and you won't hear the song
of the boy who sits on the roof
singing loud enough
his junky mother might claim him
you won't know the fear of a mother
whose youngest could be broken
because of who he was born to kiss
on the mouth
or the fear she has already broken
another son because he inherited
the madness her blood stream carries
but sure, stand here if you like

listen to my story if you like
and sure, if you like
I'll listen to yours

ACKNOWLEDGMENTS

Ampersand: "You are my favorite erection"

The Bakery: "Reality TV," "Viridian"

Bone Tax Reading Series Zine #1: "June service" (reprint), "Moist," and "Reality TV" (reprint)

Bone Tax Review: "June service"

Byline Magazine: "Small, they said"

Clapboard House: "Left staggering"

Cream City Review: "Searching for answers in the feminine hygiene aisle"

Forklift, Ohio: "Waiting for Pangaea"

Foundling Review: "Necessary fire"

Gargoyle: "River's bend"

Gertrude: "Spring tide" and "In Montecavolo, Italy there's a bank filled with cheese"

H_NGM_N: "Witness"

ILK Journal: "Hole"

Inter|rupture: "First-person shooter"

Night Train: "Saturday"

NOÖ Journal: "Note to a young friend"

Opium: "Have I been saved?"

[PANK]: "Wondering about the cancellation penalty on my cell phone"

Pear Noir!: "Thrashing"

Pearl: "Does anyone need saving?"

Pebble Lake Review: "Fear comes" and "Tuesday morning at the post
    office" (under a different title)
Potomac Review: "I don't visit gravestones" and "Circadian rhythm"
Right Hand Pointing: "Considering antiques and curiosities"
Scythe: "Grown tangled," "Family reunion," and "You wonder"
Southern Humanities Review: "This life"
Southern Women's Review: "These days are long without you," "The
    horse has gotten out again," and "Careful"
Tipton Poetry Journal: "Song for my mother"
unfold: "Ant love"
Unshod Quills: "River's Bend" (reprint)

THANKS

The people to whom I am grateful, whose support buoyed me as I walked through poetry in my middle years and for the first time, are great in number. I will likely forget to mention some folks I should not have forgotten; however, I will press on in the face of my inevitable inadequacies and send heartfelt thanks to the many who follow (and to those whose names might be missing).

First, thanks to the English Department and MFA Program at Virginia Tech and most particularly to my astonishingly supportive thesis advisors, Fred D'Aguiar, Jeff Mann, and Lucinda Roy, for three amazing years of growth, edifying challenge, and gentle handholding. Additional thanks to Bob Hicok who gave me the courage to switch from fiction to poetry and to Tom Gardner, who is perhaps the finest teacher I have ever had the pleasure of learning from. Huge thanks to all my classmates at VT (both on the MFA and Lit side), in particular those who have remained close friends as we bring who we are out of grad school and into the real world: Rob, Mark, Julia, Megan, Lamar, Omilaju, and Jeff. Sincere gratitude to my friends who are not in the poetry world and yet support with sweetness and forbearance: Jessie, Robin and my life-long love, Liz. Wild thanks to my partners in crime out here in the poetry bowl for the encouragement, love, prompting, and inspiration offered by so many including Phillip, Dena, Lynn, Ocean, Matthew, and the many writers and editors I have been lucky enough to be in company with in the Portland community and beyond as I learn and grow in poetry through my work at *Vinyl* and YesYes Books. Additional thanks to Virginia Center for the Creative Arts for time to work on this collection. Immense gratitude to everyone at Black Lawrence Press, particularly Diane Goettel for the honor of having *Necessary Fire* chosen for The St. Lawrence Book Award and for the careful treatment of the book that followed and to Alban Fischer and Christina McPhee whose cover design and cover art have pushed this book into the real.

Last but far from least, abiding love and thanks to my family. To Daniel, my partner of 30 years, the children we have raised together, Nick, James, Nicole, Charles, and Kevin, and my parents. What a life you have offered me, some of which breathes within these pages. I hope I have done it justice.

With all my love and admiration,
Katherine

KMA SULLIVAN

is the author of *Necessary Fire*, winner of the St. Lawrence Book Award from Black Lawrence Press. She co-founded *Vinyl Poetry* in 2010 and founded YesYes Books in 2011 as she was completing her MFA in poetry at Virginia Tech. She has earned fellowships in poetry and creative non-fiction from Vermont Studio Center, Virginia Center for the Creative Arts, and Summer Literary Seminars. Her poetry and essays have been published or are forthcoming in *Southern Humanities Review, The Rumpus, Forklift, Ohio, Boston Review, Gertrude, diode, Cream City Review* and elsewhere.

Earlier years were spent founding a home for teen-aged mothers, establishing a weekly tutoring program in one of Hartford's largest housing projects, earning degrees in philosophy from Trinity College and Boston College and raising five children with her partner of 30 years. She believes in the power of art and literature to improve the lives they engage.